Shadows of Soldiers Past

STEVEN LESLIE HILL

An environmentally friendly book printed and bound in England by
www.printondemand-worldwide.com

Mixed Sources
Product group from well-managed forests, and other controlled sources
www.fsc.org Cert no. TT-COC-002641
© 1996 Forest Stewardship Council
FSC

PEFC Certified
This product is from sustainably managed forests and controlled sources
www.pefc.org
PEFC
PEFC/16-33-415

This book is made entirely of chain-of-custody materials

FastPrint Publishing

www.fast-print.net/store.php

SHADOWS OF SOLDIERS PAST

A catalogue record for this book is available from the British Library

ISBN 978-178035-727-0

First published 2013 by
FASTPRINT PUBLISHING
Peterborough, England.

FOREWORD

BY

TONY HIGTON

CHAIRMAN
NOTTINGHAM & NOTTINGHAMSHIRE VICTORIA CROSS COMMITTEE

It was just prior to working on a Victoria Cross memorial to the 14 VCs cremated at Golders Green Crematorium, early in 2013, that I asked Steve to write a poem for the Service of Dedication, Steve went further and wrote 3 poems for the occasion, and was kind enough to travel to London to recite all 3 of them on the day.

War poems have been an integral part of conflicts for many years, covering all aspects of the battles fought, and there consequences, for both the military and the civilian populations.

War poets of any generation, writing about any conflict; help the population at large by creating an understanding and appreciation of what has taken place.

The experiences of those portrayed in this book reflect the deep emotions felt by those men, often the most unassuming of people quietly living their lives, often not wanting to talk about their experiences.

For many young men from Britain, going to war, sometimes seemed a romantic adventure, this was soon dispelled, as the realisation of war engulfed them, be it a nerve racking bombardment, the snipers bullet or an IED (Improvised Exploding Devise)

This excellent book looks at the many different conflicts which have taken place in our recent history, and attempts to give an accurate insight of the feelings of those men, not always an easy task, but one which has been captured by Steve Hill in this book.

The book takes a detailed look at various service personnel involved in the various conflicts, and brings them and their experiences to life, in poetry, and also telling us their personal stories, thus giving us an insight into the character and type of people they are.

In this book Steve has moved forward from his previous two books "Poems of World War One" and "Tears for the Fallen" both of which were superb, in illustrating the various aspects of the Great War in a way everyone could appreciate, to the various aspects of more recent conflicts, in which he again captures the emotions of these unassuming men who were serving our country.

Steve has preserved the colloquialisms and the language used by the interviewees, to reflect the oral record from time period of the events.

There have been many books of war poetry, and stories published over the years, which are not always easy to understand, Steven Hills book is a compelling read, giving an insight into the experiences of various members of our armed forces, which is written in a way that is sympathetic to those involved, and in a manner which the reader will be able to understand.

Tony Higton
Chairman of the Nottingham and
Nottinghamshire Victoria Cross Committee

ACKNOWLEDGEMENTS

I would like to express my sincere gratitude to the following who have helped to make this book possible.

Tony Higton	Chairman	Nottingham & Nottinghamshire Victoria Cross Committee	Foreword to this book
Robert Hann	Author	'Operation Galia' S.A.S. Behind Enemy Lines and various Children's and Professional Law Books.	For kindly allowing me to use extracts from his award winning book about his father's service with the S.A.S. in Italy during WWII
Roy Cornwell	Ex Royal Signals		For kindly allowing me to use extracts from his brother's memoirs during WWII

The following for their personal accounts of life as front line combatants and their contribution to this book:

Sergeant Nathan Cumberland	Grenadier Guards
Private Christopher Stewart	Sherwood Forresters Regiment
Corporal Stanley Hann	Special Air Service (S.A.S.)
Private Barry Brown	Royal Lincolnshire Regiment

Sergeant Christopher Black	Royal Marines
Corporal Leslie Cornwell	Durham Light Infantry
Guardsman Steven Mark Hill	Grenadier Guards
Sapper Ashley Carlin	Royal Engineers
Lance Corporal 'Gee' Gwardzinski	Royal Military Police Corps
Trooper Malcolm Shaw	9th Royal Lancers

Fast Print Publishing	Worldwide Publishers	All printing and publishing
Susan Hill	"The Boss"	Typing, initial layout, proof reading and support and love always

INTRODUCTION

Few nations on earth have such a long tradition as the armed forces of the United Kingdom. These very islands have been forged from over a thousand years of conflict, both here and around the world.

As an island race, the make-up of our people and our culture has been brought about by many historic factors. Romans, Celts, Normans, Anglo-Saxons, Danes and Vikings have all played their part in its rich and diverse history and whether we like it or not, the present trend of mass immigration to these shores is set to change the complexity of this nation once more.

Over the last thousand years, many nations have jostled for world power and between them, all have left both good and bad legacies. The United Kingdom is no exception. We once ruled three quarters of the globe through colonialism and fought other powerful countries to keep it that way. Thankfully, those days are in the past and the world is a far different place today.

No sane, rational human being wants war or conflict, but it seems that for one reason or another, war is a constant shadow in the lives of all who inhabit this planet, and because of this, our armed forces have a long history and knowledge in this field.

World Wars One and Two changed the face of the earth's geographical make-up for ever and introduced us to the nuclear age and international terrorism. So, the modern Army, Navy and Air Force of today is nothing like that of yesteryear and its role in the stability of the world is completely different than before.

You would need a book on its own to catalogue the rich history and heritage of these islands which has played a pivotal role in the world as we know it, and has left historical legacies, both positive and negative, over the centuries. But, through all that history, the armed forces of Great Britain have been at the very forefront of many wars and conflicts in defence of the kingdom, come what may.

From King Alfred to the present day our military are unsurpassed in the theatre of conflict and the discipline training and professionalism of our armed personnel has been woven like a thread down the centuries.

The following poems I have written are not a glorification of war or conflict, but rather a sad indictment of the madness of war and the mental and physical scars it leaves on the survivors and their families.

They also do not seek to justify the rights or wrongs of any conflict or our nation's involvement in them, but do hope to show the total waste of human life caused by war and the misery inflicted on nations and people, both as front line combatants and civilians.

They are, however, a testament to the bravery and professionalism of the British Army, Navy and Air Force and the medical and logistics personnel who have fought, and continue to fight, for the higher human ideals of freedom, tolerance, peace and democracy, and whom without, I would not be writing these words and you the reader, would not be reading them.

Also, along with these poems, you will also read a small, but significant collection of true life experiences of soldiers who have fought at the very 'sharp end' of war and conflict and some have suffered both physical and mental life changing injuries as a result. Their stories are a tribute, not only to their professionalism as soldiers, but to their courage as individuals to overcome their disabilities and make the very best of their future lives and the lives of their families.

S.L.H.

AUTHOR'S FOOTNOTE

The true life experiences of the armed forces personnel in this book are described in their own words and remain the sole copyright of each individual and cannot be reproduced without their consent.

The poems and verse, whilst being based on real life wars and conflicts, both past and present, are purely fictional and any resemblance to real life individual third parties or events are coincidence only, as is the surname and first name of the Grenadier Guardsman Steven Mark Hill to my own name. There is no family connection between us as far as we are both aware and I personally have never been a member of Her Majesty's Armed Forces. I am a military writer and poet only.

SHADOWS OF SOLDIERS PAST

Tour is over
Duty done
Guns are silent
The war is won

Reflective thoughts
Of comrades lost
Peace and freedom
At such a cost

But always remember
And be proud of your best
For you did your duty
When put to the test

For nothing in our lives
Forever lasts
Only memories and shadows
Of soldiers past

ENGLAND'S TALL SHIPS

Built from English Oak
Canvas sails and tall masts
The sailing ships of England
Maritime spirits of the past

Ark Royal at Trafalgar
To rout the enemies fleet
With a crew of English sailors
Press ganged from the street

To the lands of Australasia
Cooks **Discovery** southward bound
A mutiny on the **Bounty**
Scott's **Terra Nova** to McMurdo Sound

King Henry's **Tudor Rose**
Drake's **Golden Hind**
Endeavour, Resolution, Adventure
New lands they hope to find

Built from English Oak
Canvas sails and tall masts
These sailing ships of England
Now legends of the past

ENGLAND

1,000 YEARS OF CONFLICT

From over the continent they came
Strong as 'Offas steadfast' sword
To build a land of kings and queens
Saxons, Alfred and St. George

Hastings to Flanders Fields
Agincourt to Waterloo
A civil war, two world wars
And the bravery of 'the few'

The white cliffs of Dover
That 'Spitfires' once flew over
Crimea, Cromwell, The Light Brigade
The tomb of The Unknown Soldier

'Troubles' across the water
Churchill, 'The Iron Lady'
Jutland, The Armada, Trafalgar
And the pride of the English Navy

The Falklands and S.A.S.
The 'cold war' now all gone
Peninsula wars and South Africa
Passchendaele and the Somme

Henry, two Elizabeth's and Victoria
7/7, The Gulf, Iraq
Afghanistan, 'Desert Storm'
And the threat of terrorist attack

Over a thousand years in the making
From the Saxons 5 A.D.
It's soldiers, sailors and airmen
Protecting this nation of the free

Will it last another thousand years?
Of this I remain unsure
And will the St. George of England
Fly forever more?

A SOLDIER OF THE GREAT WAR

WWI
1914-1918

Nothing remains of me
I cannot be found
For I lie somewhere amongst
This battle scarred ground

Just another casualty
Of the Great War
Who fought for my Country
But exist no more

They carved out some words
On white marbled stone
My last resting place far from my home

But sometimes I still walk
Out there on the Somme
A ghost of the past
Now 100 years on

For I am the man
They could find no name for
And my stone simply reads
"A Soldier
of
The Great War"

FIELDS

FLANDERS FIELDS
BELGIUM

Out in the fields
Where the red poppies grow
Now no longer covered
In mud, rain and snow

No more destruction
Shell holes and wire
No more young lives
Consumed in the fire

Now the only sound
Is of bird song and bees
And the gentle leaf rustle
Of summer's green trees

For in these fields
Lie the brave and the best
A place where the fallen
Forever will rest

TUNNEL GHOSTS

LA BOISSELLE, FRANCE
WWI
PRESENT DAY ARCHEOLOGICAL SITE

We have laid here
For over 100 years
Someone, somewhere
Once cried long forgotton tears

Buried alive
In this awful place
Never to be seen again
A forgotton face

We fought with honour
At La Boisselle in France
All of us together
Killed by chance

Now the cannons no longer thunder
And the Great War belongs to the past
But with the discovery of our mortal remains
Our souls are now free at last

Dedicated to the La Boisselle Study Group, France

La Boisselle was the scene of a major tunnelling by allied forces and intense shelling by the German opposition, resulting in hundreds of allied troops being buried alive.

BATTLEFIELD GHOSTS

WWI

1914-1918

When the cemetery gates close
And all the living have gone
We dead walk again
The old battlefields of the Somme

We often meet the enemy
Those boys we used to fight
And talk about the old days
Long into the night

For here, there is no hatred
And the pain has long since gone
Now we are peaceful souls
United all as one

But we always ask the question
Why we were chosen to die
But before we find the answer
A new dawn it fills the sky

So we say Goodbye, auf Wiedersehen
And take our place of rest in gardens of stone
For the killing fields of Flanders
Will forever be our home

SHELL HOLE

WW1

1914-1918

I open my eyes
And slowly shake my head
Lying in this shell hole
They must have thought I was dead

There are cuts to my face and hands
Other than that I feel fine
But I guess I have been unconscious
For quite some time

I look at the bodies that lie around me
They all look dead
And I choke back my vomit
At the one with no head

Then I see movement
But he is not one of ours
And like me this German boy
Must have been here for hours

We look at each other
And exchange a smile
But I see from his waist down
He is in a mess, so horrible and vile

I try to help him
But where do you start
When a man lies before you
Blown half apart?

So I take him in my arms
And cradle his head
And talk to him gently
Until his eyes say he is dead

Another young life has ended
Another young life is done
Does it really matter anymore
Who lost and who won?

SOLDIERS OF LIGHT
WWI and WWII

In the darkness of war
They were God's Soldiers of light
And the courage of their spirits
Will forever burn bright

Never found wanting
When put to the test
They are the brave and the finest
Our nation's best

For gallant are these heroes
In God's heavenly sky
Where in eternal peace
Their souls now forever lie

Dedicated to all soldiers, sailors and airmen of the British Armed Forces who, along with other allied countries, freed the world from the 'darkness' of World Wars One and Two.

D DAY
6TH JUNE 1944

Cut down like corn
In the sun
Ripped and torn
By deadly machine gun
Mortar and cannon
Shot and shell
They landed that day
On the beaches of hell

Some never even
Made it ashore
Killed as the 'L Cs'
Dropped their doors
Intense fire from
Guns above
Ripping into
Bone, flesh and blood

Some pinned down
With no cover
Trying to fight
And help one another
The sea awash
In crimson red
And the floating bodies
Of the dead

With bravery and courage
These heroes won the day
A victory soured
By the price to pay
Their sacrifice helped change
The war
Their place in history
Forever assured

Private Leslie Cornwell Normandy WWII

My next attack was a night attack and that's even more confusing. Fields full of dead cattle as well as humans and the stench of dead bodies was terrible. Everywhere we went in Normandy was covered in dead bodies and the awful smell of death. I remember bullets whistling by my ears and we also ran over a minefield but I didn't know at the time. I was told weeks later by a returned wounded man, he said the dressing station was crowded with wounded from 'scav mines'.

We dug in the dark and next morning found only yards away two German armoured cars, no sign of the crews. I acquired some haircutting kit from one of them. We moved position a lot and I can't remember every detail now and, of course, it was 24 hours a day in action. We sent patrols out at night to bring in rations etc., to our positions at the front. One of the lads came back off patrol, well dragged back. He'd been hit in the stomach with machine gun bullets and died shortly after. He was one of the lads who used to have a lot of fun and was full of life – tip all the beds up on a Saturday night after a night out.

A big attack went through us to Fontenay after a noisy barrage, the big shells from such as the Warspite sounded very slow and 'wobbled' overhead. The 25pdrs were very close behind us and we could hear them firing and 4.2" mortars of the Kensington's, our own mortars being only 3". Support Battn. Kensignton's also had Vickers machine guns. I remember seeing the infantry running by our trenches into the attack through the smoke. I didn't envy them, the very word 'attack' made your mouth dry and stomach turn over.

Shortly after, we moved into Fontenay and dug in once more. There must have been hundreds of bodies, mostly Lincoln's, Royal Scots Fusiliers and Hallamshires from one of our other Brigades. We buried three in one trench so we wouldn't have to keep looking at them. There were also plenty of German bodies, mostly Hitler Youth.

Private Leslie Cornwell France WWII

There were three of us and a Sergeant. One man said "I'll fetch some ammo" for the three inch mortar we had, so off he went. The Sergeant stood up to get a better look and he was hit in the leg. He hobbled off just leaving the two of us.

They were firing Spandau's and Scheissers and I remember seeing bullets splattering into the ground, inches from my nose. One Jerry shouted "hands up Tommy". My mate then shouted "we've got him". It was getting dodgy and we had no chance. We just looked at each other, jumped up and made a run for it.

Again, I could hear bullets whistling past my ears. We dived behind a house for a breather, only to find on our left just across a country lane that the Germans were level with us. We turned to our left to fire and for some unknown reason, I had a half cock on my rifle. The first and only time I had one and I panicked for a second before I realised it. The German I aimed at didn't know how lucky he was and I hope he survived.

Anyway, they didn't notice us as they were busy advancing forward. We then had to run a bit further to the platoon at our rear. I remember jumping over a partially dug trench with a shovel and a leg in it, the body being some yards away. I think it was one of our lads called "Titch". We reached the other platoon positions and warned them. We again paused for a breather.

I well remember stepping into a doorway of a farmhouse. A man was milking a cow and he passed me a glass of milk. Seems funny stopping and drinking a glass of milk in the middle of a battle!

Private Leslie Cornwell France WWII

By the dates of those killed, it was the 3rd of July according to the Regimental history, the Battalion pulled out for a rest on the 1st July! Of course, we walked straight into it. The Germans opened up and we dived for cover and lay with the dead men. Sergeant Beamson turned round and shouted "get firing back, "except you", he said to me because I had the 38 wireless set. I dropped my head down which was touching his feet. The Company Commander came running by shouting "get out if you can". I don't know what happened then, we must have taken a direct hit. Lieutenant Prichard, Sergeant Beamson and myself were lying head to toe. They were both killed, but I didn't realise it until later. I was dazed for a minute or two and when I came to my senses, found a man from another platoon lying beside me. He had been hit in the chest and was breathing like a grunting pig. I think his name was Garner. I don't know how long he had been lying there. I put one arm under his and started dragging him back, although he kept saying "leave me". It never dawned on me to look at the Lieutenant and Sergeant. I crawled amongst the dead and remember quite clearly seeing a hand severed at the wrist with the fingers slightly bent – one of those little things that stick in your mind.

I was cursing the Germans, soaked in Garner's blood and tears were streaming down my face. I didn't know it, but I was suffering from shock. I saw a Corporal and shouted to him for help and he took over Garner. Carriers were taking the wounded away. I found some more of the platoon and was handed a drink by one of the stretcher-bearers.

Private Leslie Cornwell
France
WWII

One village we entered, called Anneulin, we came across a Frenchman pointing and trying to tell us something. I thought he was showing us German positions. We followed him to a German First World War cemetery, all black crosses. One of them read 'Kapitan A. Ball Aviator'. In the hedge bottom was a marble cross. The inscription on it read 'Captain Albert Ball VC, presented by the citizens of Nottingham'. This gave me a little 'turn' coming from Nottinghamshire and knowing all about the First World War ace. The Germans had removed it (possible so that the R.A.F. couldn't use it as a 'marker') so some mates and I duly manhandled it back onto the grave.

Corporal Stanley Hann
S.A.S
Italy WWII

At around 7.00 p.m., taking advantage of the pitch black of night, we got into position to attack the main road leading into Pontremoli. Only two heavy Vickers machine guns were unloaded to be used in the attack, both of which were sited so as to fire on fixed lines at a point where the road dropped around 50 feet on one side and a fast flowing river ran by on the other. We waited patiently for several hours. Then, as dawn began to break, we saw a long column of vehicles approaching from Pontremoli. At the same time, a battery of horse-drawn field artillery also moved towards the town from the opposite direction. Just as the two columns met, the Captain gave the order to attack. We opened up with the two heavy Vickers machine guns at a range of about 300 yards.

It was pandemonium! Vehicles caught fire, horses bolted, still chained to the artillery pieces they were pulling. Men jumped into the river to escape the tracer bullets that were raining down on them, only to come under small arms fire from the partisan forces on the flanks. The damage inflicted by the Vickers machine guns to the horses was gruesome. Some of the poor beasts were eviscerated, innards cascading across the road.

Sadly, we could see no sign of any car pompous enough to be carrying Mussolini, but that hardly mattered. We'd achieved our objective, caused mayhem and inflicted substantial casualties right in the heart of the enemy H.Q.

Corporal Stanley Hann
S.A.S
Italy WWII

The dangers for us and the Italian civilians and our comrades-in-arms, were ever present and likely to increase as we continued to tweak the Nazi tiger's tail. Partisan intelligence reports suggested that local enemy commanders, exasperated by the growing resistance, were planning a crackdown to flush out the partisans and parachutists operating in the 4th Operative Partisan Zone – the area we were operating in.

By the 11th January, despite the pilfering by the communists, we had enough supplies to recommence offensive operations. A recce party consisting of Walker Brown, Lofty Rose, Jock Shanley and Pct. Sumptor checked out the potential for further attack on Borghetto. The recce showed that the road bridge over the river L'Ago would be an ideal spot for an attack. The new fascist HQ had also been identified. Whilst our stick returned to Halifax drop zone to prepare for another drop, Lieutenant Riccomini and his men ambushed the bridge, while the remainder of the squad took up position 300 feet from the fascist HQ building in Borghetto Di Varo and make ready to attack. Ricky told me what happened later.

As the SAS got into position, two fascist soldiers started an impromptu game of tennis in the road, unaware of the imminent danger they were in. Just as the attack was about to start, a column of vehicles could be heard coming into the town square towards the smaller of the two ambush parties. Since this group had only one Bren gun, they decided to wait until the vehicles had passed to enable the larger party, which had five Bren guns, to attack the vehicles further up the road. With no radio communications this was a risky strategy but, fortunately, both the SAS sections were on the same wave-length. The main ambush party began the attack and peppered the German trucks and vehicles with Bren gun fire. The recce party joined in and opened fire from the rear. The vehicle column, which included a

British captured staff car, a ten-ton lorry full of equipment and several transporters carrying troops bound for the front, found itself suddenly the centre of a murderous cross-fire.

Corporal Stanley Hann
S.A.S
Italy WWII

As we laid there, praying, we could see the tracer bullets passing harmlessly above our heads. It was clear the enemy could not see us, but were taking a guess as to our whereabouts from the noise we were making.

There was no sense in waiting around for the mist to dissipate. On the Major's signal, we made a break for it across the field and into the woods beyond. Both machine guns continued their angry chatter as we bent low and scurried as fast as we could towards the tree line. We could hear the gunners calling out to each other in a foreign language none of us could understand. We realised we had at last come into contact with the Mongolian ski troops we had heard so much on our travels.

We reached the cover of the trees, but were by no means safe. A German soldier, smoking a cigarette, was leaning by a tree. He was so intently peering through his field glasses into the gloom to see what his colleagues were firing at that he didn't see us. As we watched, another German soldier appeared out of the mist to get a light for his cigarette from his colleague. We had no choice, but to rush them both and hope there were no others in the immediate vicinity. Lofty Rose and Sid Gargan headed for the first one. Kennedy and I went for the other.

It was all over in a second. They were both so stunned by our sudden appearance out of the mist that they didn't put up much of a fight. After a short scuffle, during which Lofty Rose banged their heads together to quieten them down, they were persuaded to 'come quietly' to meet the Major. They meekly put their hands on their heads and we marched our prisoners a few yards back to the others.

Our captives turned out to be a German Sergeant and his orderly, part of a mortar team. They had orders to open fire on Sero as soon as it got light enough to see the target. The mortar unit numbered eight men in all but their comrades, fortunately for us, took to their heels as soon as we came charging out of the mist. An additional bonus was the fact that the Sergeant had with him a vital part of the firing mechanism without which the mortars wouldn't work.

Sapper Ashley Carlin
501 Field Company Royal Engineers
56TH London Division
World War II

We trained for six months near Kirkuk, Iraq and we were then assigned to the 8th Armoured Division as Engineers and Sappers and after a period in the desert, we landed in Sicily. From there, we went to the Italian peninsular and landed at Anzio where we were to form the beachhead and try to stop supplies to Monte Casino.

The Germans gave us absolute hell on that beachhead with their machine guns and the huge cannon at Monet Casino known to us as 'Anzio Annie' which pulverized the beach constantly with its huge shells. How I managed to survive that place, I will never know.

The Americans then took over from us and we were assigned further north to break up the German supply chains and it was around a place near the River Senio that we were instructed to remove mines which had been planted by the retreating Germans along the roads etc. They were small mines, about hand size, in wooden boxes which we had to prod out of the ground with small sticks. As you can imagine, casualties in our section were high and, unfortunately, one of them was me and I lost my left leg.

Sapper Ashley Carlin
501 Field Company Royal Engineers
56TH London Division
World War II

We didn't see that many atrocities in Italy, but we did come across some Italian women's bodies that had been raped and murdered by the retreating German units.

We also had some Ghurkha's assigned to us and these were great and fearless soldiers but, like every army, there is always a bad apple or two and one of these Ghurkha's raped an Italian woman and murdered her. He was reported to the N.C.O. of the division who executed him.

Sapper Ashley Carlin
501 Field Company Royal Engineers
56TH London Division
World War II

I was called up, aged 18, in 1941 and was sent to Elgin, Scotland for six months training. On completion, I joined the 501 Field Company Royal Engineers in Bury St Edmunds as part of the 56th London Division known as the 'Black Cats' due to the regimental emblem.

After 6 weeks, we were shipped out via Capetown and Bombay and eventually disembarked at Basra, Iraq where we were put on a train to a place called Kirkuk. Our Company was on this train for about two days in cattle trucks which had slats for the sides. The train hardly stopped for the entire journey, so the only way you could answer the call of nature was to hang your 'personal bits' out through the slats and let mother nature take its course, much to the disgust of the locals who would be along the tracks and suddenly be confronted by someone's backside or other 'letting it all go'.

It wasn't the nicest way to introduce yourself to the locals, but as they say, 'when you have to go, you've got to go'.

'THE FEW'

BATTLE OF BRITAIN
1940
WWII

They flew from 'Maidstone'
By dawns early light
The 'White Cliffs' of the coastline
Coming into sight

Moving into position
And looking down below
There were the 'Heinkels'
Flying row on row

Heading for London
To deliver their load
With '109' escorts up front
Leading their nose

Now in attack formation
And coming in from the sun
The 'Spitfires' are ready
The Battle of Britain has just begun

Into the enemy
From all sides
This is a dogfight
There's nowhere to hide

Rapid fire
Bullets fly
Enemy bombers
Explode in the sky

The '109's

Put the 'Spits' to the test
But once again
The Spitfire's best

In this death game
Played in the sky
The rules are simple
But the stakes are high

And in our country's 'Darkest Hour'
Victory it came through
With the power of the 'Spitfire'
And the bravery of 'The Few'

VICTORIA CROSS

I am the cross of valour
Given to the finest and the brave
For extreme courage under fire
And the comrade's lives they saved

For in the intense heat of conflict
As the battle it raged higher
They sacrificed their own lives
In wars burning flames of fire

And on the roll call of honour
Their names will forever be etched on me
For I am the cross of valour
The Victoria Cross, V.C.

Dedicated to all the recipients of the Queens highest award 'for valour' in the face of the enemy, and to the Nottingham and Nottinghamshire Victoria Cross Committee and the Victoria & George Cross Society, whose charitable contributions help highlight the immense gallantry of these men and women.

THE COLD WAR

Yuri was born in '48
A cold war child
Of the Soviet state

Raised and taught
The communist way
Told what to think
He learned what to say

Now he plays
The nuclear game
'Mutual Assured Destruction'
Totally insane

Launch codes at the ready
Keys in place
Waiting for the 'West's'
First mistake

The missiles are ready
The launch is on
The Armageddon code
'Defcon One'

But this time
It's only a 'drill'
To see how quick
Each side can kill

As for Yuri
In the silo's deep
He's just a number
In the cold war 'heat'

Private Barry Brown
1st Battalion Royal Lincolnshire Regiment
Malaya 1955-1957

A report came through to our H.Q. that lights had been seen intermittently shining on a rough jungle pathway approximately 5 miles from base.

The duty platoon was scrambled and moved to the area and set up an ambush to kill or capture the suspected communist rebels which were assumed to be coming towards our lines. The Second Lieutenant in charge organised the men into position and was checking that everyone was in place when the suspected communists as they got closer suddenly realised that they were about to be caught in a trap and duly panicked and started to run into the jungle.

This sparked off some of our men in the waiting platoon and they started firing at the fleeing insurgents. Unfortunately, the Second Lieutenant was in the line of fire and was accidentally killed by his own men. As it turned out, the suspected communists were, in actual fact, Malayan Home Guard who were on our side and had been out hunting deer in the jungle.

Private Barry Brown
1st Battalion Royal Lincolnshire Regiment
Malaya 1955-1957

As you can imagine, the toilet facilities in a tropical jungle were primitive to say the least. They consisted of a trench about 3 feet wide and 12 feet deep over which some wooden boards were laid across and a small wooden hut about the size of a garden shed would be fixed on top. Inside was a seat with a hole in the middle where you sat down over the exposed pit to do your business. You literally had to hold your breath when having a 'crap' as the stench from weeks and months of excreta and urine was overwhelming and made you feel physically sick , not to mention the jungle wildlife that lived in there. So, you didn't hang around long, believe me.

Trooper Malcolm Shaw
9th Royal Lancers
West Germany
1955

I started my time in West Germany during the 'cold war', as it was then known, as a driver in Mark 1 Centurion Tanks. I was also learning to be the wireless operator as all Centurions had a four man crew which consisted of driver, gun operator, wireless operator and C.O. (Commanding Officer). We all had to learn another skill so in the event of several tank crew members being injured or killed, we could still assemble a complete crew.

On this certain occasion, we were training near the border and I was loading the shell into the breach of the gun. There is a trip mechanism which stops the shell being accidentally fired and I forgot to remove it. I said "fire" to the gunner, but nothing happened. We tried again and still nothing happened. So we now had a 20lb live shell still in the breach.

The C.O. stopped the tank and ordered everyone out except me until I had released the trip mechanism by hand and we then carried on our way. We went through the procedure again and to all my crew member's dismay, I panicked and 'cocked up' again with the same result as before.

The C.O. was so bloody angry that he 'walloped' me with an oil dipstick which was hung on the side of the tank and, worse still, due to my error the entire tank exercise was halted until I again sorted it out, much to my embarrassment.

Lance Corporal Zbiegniew Gwardzinski
Royal Corp's Military Police
West Germany

We were on exercise in West Germany, as it was then known before the fall of the Berlin Wall, and were attached to the Royal Artillery at the time.

The Commanding Officer, who was a Major, asked to see me. When I arrived at his office, he asked me my name and I replied 'Lance Corporal Gwardzinski, Sir'.

He replied 'how do you spell that Lance Corporal?'

I said 'Sir, if you take all the letters of the alphabet, put them in a bag, give them a good shake and throw them on the table, that would be it'.

'OK', he replied. 'From now on, I will call you Lance Corporal Alphabet'.

THE WALL
BERLIN
1960s

A 'curtain' of iron
Concrete and steel
This wall of indifference
To the free spirit we feel

And inside that wall
You are a product of the state
Where you are watched and monitored
For any mistake

No personal freedom
And as a person, no longer exist
Only a number, comrade
On the Soviet list

For the state rules all
That's the socialist way
So tow the party line
And you may live another day

But the more you supress the spirit
And try to extinguish its flame
The more it will burn brightly
In freedoms name

THE TROUBLES
BELFAST
1970s

In a city divided
Communities torn apart
Bombs and random violence
Had ripped out Belfast's heart

The Protestants on the 'Shankill'
Catholics on the 'Falls'
With Para-Militaries on both sides
Fighting for their cause

Irish killing Irish
As hatred fanned the flames
All this death and destruction
Carried out in God's name

And in the middle were the soldiers
Not really knowing why
It seemed the British Government
Had only sent them there to die

Freedom Fighters or Terrorists?
Both Loyalists and Provo's too
And a British Army of occupation?
It seemed there was nothing no one could do

But at last The 'Good Friday' Agreement
Gave this city back its heart
With common sense on all sides
To begin a fresh, new start

So for the present and future generations

On all sides of the divide
Let us pray the period known as
'The Troubles'
As at last finally died

Private Christopher Stewart Worcestershire & Sherwood Forresters Regiment Northern Ireland 1972

We started our tour of the province in 1972 and within 3 weeks after arriving and getting to know the area via foot patrols etc., we were deployed to Londonderry City Centre.

On 16th April that year, we received a call that some teenagers were trying to break into the main water supply pumping station which distributed mains water to the Police and Army H.Q. and Barracks. So our foot patrol was deployed to monitor the situation.

On arrival at the corner of William Road and Sackville Street, our Corporal William (Bill) Cashmore went forward to observe these teenagers. I was probably no more than 4 to 5 metres behind him in a doorway and was operating the patrol radio. Corporal Cashmore came back to me and asked if I would carry on monitoring what they were doing while he radioed H.Q. and briefed them on the situation. I was at this point directly on the corner of the two streets and covered to the rear by Corporal Cashmore and to my right across the street by Pt. Peter Haywood.

At that moment, I suddenly had a thundering pain in my right thigh and found myself flying into the street gutter, smashing my jaw and head in the process as I fell.

Corporal Cashmore screamed at me to “pull in your weapon” as the momentum of the fall had moved it away from my body, although it was still attached to my wrist by the rifle sling. It all happened so fast, probably only seconds or half a minute, but to me it seemed an age as the pain was so intense in my right thigh.

Corporal Cashmore ran from his position and grabbed me and my weapon and dragged me via my flack vest into the relative safety of a house doorway. He immediately called for back-up on the radio and

Pt. Haywood ran across the street and to our position and immediately began to administer battlefield dressings to the wound in my right thigh at which point I subsequently passed out unconscious.

Corporal Cashmore had also during his attempt to rescue me from the open street position in which I lay took a bullet to his right leg while standing to try and cover me.

The next recollection I have is being in an armoured personnel carrier known as a 'pig' to us soldiers roaring its way to the local hospital. Inside the 'pig' Corporal DeBarry was giving me mouth to mouth resuscitation to keep me alive and I can honestly say that both he and Corporal Cashmore both saved my life that day.

On arrival at the hospital, I was unconscious, but still alive and the staff soon ascertained the extent of my injury and I was immediately flown by helicopter to Belfast City Hospital. I was, at this stage, in and out of consciousness and eventually awoke to find my parents at my bedside as they had been flown from Brize Norton in England to Belfast straight away. I did not know what had actually happened to me at that stage so my parents and later the hospital doctor explained that I had been shot in the upper right thigh by an I.R.A. Sniper using a 'dum dum' bullet which is when the point of the bullet is removed and a sawn cut is made in the remaining lead capping which causes it to shatter on impact and cause extensive damage to the victim.

Some fragments had exited my body via my backside and right knee, but the main body of the bullet had torn 4 inches of bone from my right femur and had severed my femoral artery. As I looked at my right leg, it was about five times the size of my undamaged left leg due to the swelling. I was, at this point, on a public general ward in the hospital. This was not an ideal situation to be in so they quickly moved me to a side ward where I was guarded 24 hours by the 2nd Parachute Regiment.

At first, all went well with my recovery, so in May they moved me back to a hospital in England. Here, I underwent several operations and was on traction for a considerable time, but nothing seemed to be working and I eventually developed a gangrene blood disorder in the leg which started to show signs of moving into my upper body.

This deteriorated rapidly over the coming weeks and months and around July, I lost my big toe which quite simply dropped off on a visit to the toilet in my wheelchair. By early August, I had deteriorated to such extent that the doctor advised myself and my parents that amputation was the only option left. Without it, I would probably die within one week.

At that point, the then Prime Minister, Edward Heath, was walking around the hospital chatting to wounded soldiers etc., with some of the military 'top brass' when he approached my parents who had just been informed of my dilemma. My Father told him in no uncertain terms to 'piss off'. That very afternoon, I had my right leg removed and thus began my life as an amputee on 8th August 1972.

Guardsman Steven Mark Hill
Grenadier Guards
Londonderry, Northern Ireland 1970's

On our very first day in the province, I was driving a Land Rover with a Sergeant and three more Guardsman with another Land Rover behind us. As we turned at the junction of a street, we came under sniper fire. We immediately pulled over the vehicles and jumped out to return fire. The lad who was driving the other Land Rover crouched down beside his vehicle when a bullet from the sniper hit the road, bounced of the ankle of his boot and cut straight across the skin of his buttocks, burning his trousers and backside. We all had to pick him up and lay him face down in the Land Rover as he could not sit on his burnt backside, much to his annoyance and our laughter.

Guardsman Steven Mark Hill
Grenadier Guards
Northern Ireland 1970s

We received a call that there was some suspicious activity in the main part of town near a bank, so our unit was dispatched to investigate. I was driving a Land Rover at the time and as we approached the area, two youths suddenly started running down the street. At that precise moment, there was an almighty explosion and both lads were blown to pieces. It was later ascertained that they were para military and had accidentally blown themselves up with their own bomb.

Guardsman Steven Mark Hill
Grenadier Guards

Myself and a fellow Guardsman were on sentry duty at St James's Palace in London on a bitter cold winters evening in 1974 and were at the rear gates of the palace. At about 10.00 p.m., the door at the rear opened and a little old lady came out with a tray which had two tots of brandy on it. She brought them over to us and said that it was a terribly cold night and thought the brandy would warm us up. We drank them down and thanked her very much and she bid us 'goodnight'.

It was then we both realised that it was Her Majesty the Queen Mother.

RIOT

BELFAST
1970s

Patrolling along
In random file
The locals watch us
Without a smile

We turn a street corner
An angry mob is up ahead
Bricks and bottles
Now fly over our heads

Targets of hate
The adrenalin's high
Burning vehicle smoke
Now fills the sky

Acrid stench
From a burning tyre
A colleague's down
His clothes on fire

Officer's order
'Baton' rounds hit home
As we take 'hits'
From bricks and stone

Then the rioters disperse
And are now away
Belfast with the army
It's just another day

SEASONS PASS
NORTHERN IRELAND
1970s

Seasons pass
They come and go
Sun and rain
Wind and snow

But here on Ulster's streets
Each day is just the same
In this place of random violence
We play the survival game

All we want
Is for these damned troubles to end
To go back home to England
To our families and friends

No more pain and bloodshed
No more widows tears
No more mindless hatred
Passed down through the years

A final end
To this 'bloody' sectarian war
Just a life of peace
Like we had before

But I have a strange feeling
That it will never be
For somewhere there's a bullet
And I feel it's waiting for me

MOMENT IN TIME
FALKLAND'S WAR

They put what was left of me
In a black plastic bag
My coffin now draped
In the Union Flag

A volley of gunfire
A bugle sound
My family's tears
As I am lowered down

Bible in hand
The Reverend says
'Ashes to Ashes'
Over my grave

And as my soul now leaves
Deaths dark night
The angels wait
By the tunnel of light

For life's journey never really ends
And our spirits, they never die
For this moment here in time
Is but a brief goodbye

Sergeant Christopher Black
Royal Marines
The Falklands War 1982

It has been said that there are such things as just wars, even though there is no such thing as a good war. And I firmly believe that this was a just war – for Britain. It's also a time to reflect on what happened, politically. Like many wars, this one could have, and should have been avoided. At least lord Carrington and a couple of his junior ministers had the decency to resign, although whether they were really the ones that made the mistakes, I cannot say.

I suppose because I had served previously in the Falklands and I knew the people and the history, I had no doubts about the rightness of what we were doing. Paradoxically, I believe that Britain has no more right to claim sovereignty over the islands than the Argentineans without the consent of the people who live there. To my mind, the islands belong to the people. I believe all people have the right to self-determination and to decide under which flag and sovereign government they live.

At that time, I had relatives living in Argentina and had some awareness of what life was like for ordinary Argentineans under the fascist dictatorship of Galtierri. I could only guess what might happen if the "Dirty War", Argentina's ultimate solution to the problem of "left-wing" terrorism (which was a sinister, murderous campaign against ideas and beliefs) was turned on the islanders.

Sergeant Christopher Black
Royal Marines
The Falklands War 1982

On the 2nd May came the news of the sinking of the Belgrano. I don't remember there being any jubilation, but a lot of sympathy for the more than 320 poor Argentinian sailors who died. If that event made us feel a little less comfortable then two days later the sinking of HMS Sheffield invoked a very sombre mood. The south Atlantic is a cold and unforgiving ocean.

We landed in the very early hours of the 21st May, got wet feet and yomped off into the hills above San Carlos. Our initial mission was to defend the beachhead so that all the stores etc., that would allow the land forces to do the job could be unloaded. An attack was expected from ground forces – that is what the Argentineans should have done. Thankfully, they didn't, but did attack us daily with their air force and took a terrible toll.

Sergeant Christopher Black
Royal Marines
The Falklands War 1982

The air raids continued, and then one day I got a call on the field telephone from a corporal in a forward o.p. (observation post) to say that they'd taken an Argentine pow. A Gunner (Royal Artillery spotter) attached to the marines had gone to *answer the call of nature* and returned quickly to the marine corporal in charge of the o.p. to tell him that there was *"some bloke laying over there in a different uniform to us"*. The corporal grabbed another marine and with the Gunner went and captured the Argentine marine officer who was a forward air controller (FAC); he had been directing the enemy aircraft onto our positions and, more devastatingly, the ships that anchor in San Carlos Waters which became known as Bomb Ally. We lost some good lads during those first few days. Lads that died at their posts firing GPMGs from slit trenches at the attacking Argentine air force A4 Skyhawkes and Super Etendardes.

Sergeant Christopher Black
Royal Marines
The Falklands War 1982

Some time later we moved to take up new positions. On arrival we needed to register our mortars. This means selecting targets, normally ground where you might expect an attack to come from, and firing a couple of mortar rounds on to the selected target. Once you have registered targets it is easier to direct the fire to other targets using the registered target as a reference. Well, we fired two rounds to register the first target and as the smoke cleared, this Argentinean soldier stood up and put his arms in the air. I don't know who was more surprised, him or us. It was like a scene from a Carry On film. The poor bloke, who had become detached from his comrades, could not have picked a worse place to lay low. We went and picked him up and he informed us where the rest of his section was. We went looking for them and after a short exchange of fire, they also gave up.

Sergeant Christopher Black
Royal Marines
The Falklands War 1982

Over the years following the conflict, we learned of the other casualties; those with emotional and mental health problems which would not have been evident at that time. 255 British lives were lost during the conflict, but it is estimated the same number have since taken their own lives due to PTSD. Our political leaders really need to be aware when they commit our forces to combat that not all casualties will have physiological injuries. Mental images of war can haunt people for many years, for the rest of one's life. Provision to help such victims must be made available.

A SEA OF TEARS
FALKLAND ISLANDS

The night is black
And the cold wind it moans
We lay a thousand miles
From the comfort of our homes

And battered by the elements
Our headstones proudly stand
For we all now rest here
In this cold, hard land

We all fought with dignity,
Courage and pride
Comrades in arms together
Now forever side by side

And the future generations of these islands
Will remember us down the years
When we gave them back their freedom
And the sea washed this land with tears

THE REGIMENT
FALKLAND'S WAR

The 'Sea King' touches down
And we all hit the ground
The pilot gives the thumbs up
And in seconds it's a distant sound

We all go night vision
And check the terrain and sky
Every muscle in our bodies
Now pumped with adrenalin high

I check our co-ordinates
Then without a sound
Our patrol starts 'tabbing'
Across the Falkland's ground

Reaching our destination
We engage the enemy and fight
Then as quickly as we appeared
We disappear like ghosts in the night

The 'Sea King' again touches down
And I give the pilot the thumbs up high
In moments, we are just a memory
As we disappear into the dawn sky

For we are 'The Regiment'
Special Forces, Britain's elite
As we melt into the sunrise
Another covert mission complete

A SOLDIER'S PRIDE

BALKAN'S CONFLICT
SAREJAVO

Standing on a street corner
Rifle in my hand
Just a 'peace keeping' soldier
In a war torn land

Serbians and Croatians
Fighting for each side
While we NATO soldiers
Try to bridge the religious divide

A snipers shot rings out
And I am the man that's going down
A victim of mindless violence
As I hit the streets hard ground

A simple statistic
In this crazy war
Just one more soldier
Who will never walk anymore

For they tried to take my life
And wished that I had died
But one thing they can never take
Is this proud soldier's pride

FRESH BREAD IN THE SAND
IRAQ
ALLIED CHECKPOINT

'Halt', I cried as she walked toward me
Her arms open wide
I lifted up my weapon
Which was hanging by my side

Covered from head to toe
In a Burka they all wear
She seemed to know no danger
Either that, or did not care

And as she came closer
I took a 'bead' with my gun
A few more steps nearer
And her life would soon be done

I could now see the bag
She held at her side
And as I took aim
'Please stop', again I cried

My finger squeezed the trigger
And the round it hit home
Tearing through her chest
Splintering flesh and bone

I ran across to her body
To check the bomb in her hand
All I found to my horror
Was fresh bread in the sand

And now she comes to see me
Each night in my dreams
In this world where I now live
Full of tortured screams

DUST AND SAND

AFGHANISTAN

Another explosion
Another death
Another day
In this tangled mess

Another day
Just like before
Another killing
In this senseless war

Another statistic
On a government chart
Another family
With a broken heart

Another brave soldier
In a politicians war
Does anybody know
What we are fighting for?

And when it's all over
Will there be peace in this land?
Or just be blown in the wind
Like dust and sand?

I.E.D.CENTRAL
SANGIN
AFGHANISTAN

'I.E.D. Central'
The sign it read
Where you lose your legs
Or end up dead

For the next six months
Until the tour is done
Endless patrols
Under a white hot sun

A cat and mouse game
To see whose best
Everyday our skills
Are put to the test

But in this game
The threshold is high
One mistake and it's
Hello, goodbye

Never really knowing whose friend or foe
The days and weeks
Seem to pass so slow

Feel like I am walking
On life's thin ledge
With mind and body
On a razors edge

Body armour and helmet
Seem to weigh a ton

With dry mouthed anticipation
I patrol with my gun

For each day out here
You must learn very fast
For in I.E.D. Central
It may be your last

Sangin is a town in the province of Helmand, Afghanistan, but is commonly referred to by serving soldiers as I,E.D. Central (Improvised Explosive Device) due to the amount of causalities resulting from these deadly weapons which are designed to maim and kill

Sergeant Nathan Cumberland Grenadier Guards/3rd Parachute Regiment Afghanistan

In October 2009, I was on my third tour of duty in Hellmand Province, Afghanistan with the Grenadier Guards.

On this particular day, my section was required to give cover to a team of Royal Engineers who had discovered what they had thought was some I.E.D's and bomb making equipment. As we walked into a grassed area, there was a terrific explosion and I suddenly found myself lying alone in a bomb crater.

At first, I didn't realise it was me who had been blown up, but as I looked down at my lower body, the full horror of what had happened sank in. My right leg looked like a tank had run over it and was crushed from the knee down, and my left leg was about 2 metres from me hanging in the surrounding vegetation.

We immediately came under fire from the Taliban and, as Section Commander, I instructed my platoon to engage the enemy while at the same time, trying to stop the intense bleeding from my legs.

Assistance was immediately called and my men put down heavy suppressing fire. The unit medic tried to inject me with morphine, but in the noise and confusion, accidently injected himself.

Eventually, I received the morphine and was medivacked out of the fire fight. It was later ascertained that I had been the bombers target as I was the Section Leader, and the young Afghan teenager who had triggered the explosive device was killed along with several of his Taliban colleagues by the soldiers in my unit.

As a result of my injuries, I lost the lower part of my left leg below the knee and my right leg above the knee, and from 2009 to 2012, when I left the army, I have spent recovering and learning to walk again with the aid of prosthetic limbs.

POLITICIANS

Never give a straight answer
So called defenders of the free
They just feed you lies
While stealing a nation's liberty

Tax you to death
And beyond if they could
But be sure they will tell you
It's for your own good

Put on a smile
And a patriotic show
Feed you information
Only the state wants you to know

They send you off to war
In a different place
But the enemy is the enemy
Just a different face

And the politician's, as usual
Remain at the rear
While you're at the front
With a 'gut' full of fear

They watch you bleed
While their 'snouts' are in the trough
And it doesn't really matter
If a few of you are lost

So they order another fine meal
'Who cares about the dead'
Of course, it's washed down
With a nice 'Chateaux vin red'

And back home satellites and cameras
Watch for every mistake
Are you fighting for the free
Or is the enemy really the state?

What happened to liberty and justice
Are they forever a thing of the past?
And freedom of information
How long will that last?

LONG DARK TUNNEL
AFGHANISTAN

Back from Afghanistan
I've finished my tour
But the man that went there
Is not here anymore

For I left something
Out there in the sun
And I feel like I'm looking
Down the barrel of a gun

Just a long, dark tunnel
With no light at the end
No one to talk to
Or be my friend

Days pass to weeks
And weeks to months
As I sit in the local bar
With the old town drunks

An image flashes
Into my mind
Of fellow soldiers torn apart
By a road land mine

In slow motion
Like on a big screen
Images of death
In some endless scream

Then at night I see faces
Of friends and foe
It's like my own living
Macabre death show

So I sleep and I drink
And I drink some more
Constantly stuck in this nightmare's
Revolving door

When will it all end
Who can say
But I hope I don't wake up again
To another new day

SCORCHED RAGS
IRAQ & AFGHANISTAN

The very first time
That you see the dead
Their faces are forever etched
Inside your head

Torn, hot metal
Muscle and bone
They lie here in pieces
So far from home

They were some widow's husband
Some mother's son
Now just 'scorched rags'
Under a white hot sun

So take a good look
Blair, Bush and Brown
This is forever your legacy
You political clowns

FINAL TOUR OF DUTY
AFGHANISTAN

I once lived life
But now I am gone
Blown apart
By a roadside bomb

No more laughter
Or life of the young
For this tour of duty
Is now forever done

So look after my boy
And my little princess
And know, my darling
You were simply the best

You gave me true love
All my short life
A beautiful lady
A mother and wife

And you were my inspiration
On whom I could always depend
And the sadness cuts deep
At this terrible end

But try to remember
All the good times past
For nothing in our mortal lives
Forever lasts

For the angels are now here
And I must say goodbye
For all of us one day
Must eventually die

But know I will wait for you
Until your life's end
Goodbye my sweet love
My true best friend

THE DARKNESS

POST TRAUMATIC STRESS SYNDROME

At night they stand
At the foot of my bed
Their distorted faces
Forever etched inside my head

I try to sleep
As I toss and turn
But all I see
Is the scorched earth burn

People on fire
Both friend and foe
Tormented souls
In my own death show

I wash my hands
But can't erase the blood
Chain gun whine
And artillery thud

The air is full
Of cordite and smoke
My comrades on fire
Forever scream and choke

Hot metal shrapnel
Embedded in their bodies and head
Limbs torn off
In this carnage of the dead

I am lost in spirit
And broken in mind
Where do I begin
How do I find

The door to escape
The darkness I am in
I can see a light
But it shines so dim

So I lie here alone
As I shiver and shake
'Please someone help me'
'Please for God's sake'

AFTER THE DARKNESS

When life is hard
And the road seems long
When you feel weak
And the problem seems strong

When you feel like a ship
Tossed on the sea
The storm is raging
And you want to be free

When the tears come easy
And you are torn inside
When the world seems cruel
And you want to hide

Just remember life is like a season
It comes and it goes
Sometimes it rains
And sometime it snows

But after the darkness
There must come light
That's when at last
You can win the fight

So learn from the mistakes
You have done
And unravel the tight threads
Life has spun

For victory is around the corner
Just over the hill
With the strength of your soul
And the power of your will

COMING HOME
IRAQ

I step down onto the station platform
To the cheering crowds gathered there
But they will all never know
The thoughts we soldiers share

For I have been to Iraq
That 'Hell hole' in the sun
Where sudden death awaits you
Before each day is done

There I have witnessed bloodshed
Across this sun scorched land
And seen the lifeless bodies
Lying broken in the sand

But now I return to England
This land I love so dear
No more endless foot patrols
And stomach churning fear

And there she is waiting
With a smile and arms held open wide
As I push my way through the crowds
To hold her at my side

And so I kiss her lovingly
With tears of joy and pain
And hope I can find the man I used to be
And become myself again

DEAR PRIME MINISTER
WOOTTON BASSETT

I remember standing there
In that small town place
And asking where you were
As the tears ran down my face

And as they carried him by me
The only son I had ever known
His coffin draped in the Union Flag
Of the country he once called home

For you sent him to a place
Out in the burning sun
"Have you any idea, Mr Blair
What it's like to lose your son?"

And you couldn't even be bothered
To turn up for his return
Probably too busy, I guess
Counting the 'millions' that you earn

And as I look at my boy
One of England's best
I think of your grinning face
Just a clown, like all the rest

FURTHER ON UP THE ROAD

During our lives
We will all cross that line
All of us some day
Must finish our time

For on the pathway of life
Like a field of war
A battle commences
Like centuries before

But before the whistle blows
And your time is done
Pause for reflection
On the course you have run

For it may seem unforgiving
And at times unfair
But you're here for a reason
That's why you are there

So at the next crossroads
As you struggle with life's load
Just remember there's a new dawn
Further on up the road

DEAR JESUS
LONDON
7/7

Dear Jesus
I was only little
When the 'bad men'
Came that day

They hurt and took
My daddy
And made him
Go away

He said goodbye to mummy
As he finished his breakfast tea
Then quickly gave a kiss
To my big sister and me

He caught the red bus
That takes him to work
And that's when the 'bad men'
Came and made daddy hurt

But mummy says he's with you now
And is happy as can be
But I don't want him there
I want him back here with me

So dear Jesus will you help me
And please send my daddy home
Because I am so sad
And fed up of being alone

Harry
Aged 7

D DAY GHOSTS
NORMANDY, FRANCE
PRESENT DAY

Wet mist shrouds
The cold, hard night
The unforgiving sea
Bathed in clear moonlight

Deserted roads
And winters leafless trees
The scent of the sea
Carries on the breeze

And down on the beach
The angry sea crashes its waves
Hard rolling breakers,
Awash in misty haze

And up on the headland
The gun emplacements stand
These fortresses of war
Built by hand

It's on a night like this
So the locals say
You can hear the landing crafts
That beached that day

The noise and gun fire
And screams of men
As shot and shell
Tore into them

The heroes of the landings
They were that day
Their ghosts still here
Forever to stay

LIFE'S JOURNEY

Life is like a journey
Down a long train track
With one destination
And no ticket back

A one way trip
To the Promised Land
A beautiful heaven
Or the place of the damned

You pay the fare
In blood, sweat and tears
As the pain cuts deep
Through the long, hard years

Some reach their station
And never look back
Others de-rail
And come off track

Some find love
And have a true friend
Others walk forever
Down a long dead end

Some spend a life
Of hell on earth
Others judge a person
By their monetary worth

Some are rich
Some are poor
Others never find the key
To open life's door

Some search forever
All in vain
Others wander the darkness
And go insane

Some judge a person
By the colour of their skin
Others waste their lives
In vice and sin

For life is a mixture
Of good and bad
Some are happy
Others are sad

But one thing is for certain
As the train rounds the bend
There is one final station
And it's called 'The End'

ARMISTICE DAY

Out in the fields
Summer to autumn yields
And leafless trees now sway
Time to remember the fallen
It's Armistice Day

In once these fields that roared with thunder
Lay the remains of many a good man under
This earth torn so hard
Drenched in blood
And long since battle scarred

But today on the hour we will remember
These brave souls now all gone
Of their sacrifice and courage
May forever their memory
Always live on

ROYAL BRITISH LEGION

They march along
Heads held high
Medals worn
And banners fly

To pay respect
To the fallen dead
The sacrifice made
And the blood they shed

Stand to attention
The 'Last Post' sounds
A minute of silence
On this hallowed ground

Ceremony over
Wreath's are laid
May their memory live always
And never fade

The Legion forever
The soldier's friend
On which so many
Still depend

So shoulder to shoulder
Branch standard's fly
Together for the fallen
With heads held high

EPILOGUE

The poetry and personal recollections in this book are, I think, beautifully encapsulated in the moving and poignant words of Sergeant Christopher Black on reflection of his service with the Royal Marines during the Falkland Islands conflict, and say everything about the sadness and pain at the loss of fellow friends and comrades in arms.

Every one of our lads that didn't come home had a mum, a dad, a sister, brother, wife or child. I want the nation to remember not just the fallen, but also those who were bereaved. To those families I would say "we remember them as they were. We talk of them still, not the manner of their passing, but the things they did before that time, of the experiences we shared with them, our brothers-in-arms who remain forever young". One thing is sure,

WE WILL REMEMBER THEM

POPPIES

Where they have fallen
We will grow
On this scarred battlefield
Where the four seasons blow

Our stems stand tall
To the memory of the dead
Our petals the colour
Of the blood that they shed

So if their mortal remains
Are never found or given a final grave
Then forever we will mark the place
Of the passing of the brave

FURTHER READING AND MILITARY CHARITIES

Tears for the Fallen 1914-1918	Steven Leslie Hill	ISBN-978-178035-471-2 Fast Print Publishing www.fast-print.net
Poems of World War One 1914-1918	Steven Leslie Hill	ISBN-978-1-908336-10-1 Menin House Publications www.tommiesguides.co.uk

Signed copies of the above two books can be obtained from stevenlesliehill@btinternet.com

Operation 'Galia' S.A.S. Behind Enemy Lines Italy WWII	Rob Hann	www.hannbooks.com
Distant Deeds 1914-1918	Tim Priestley	www.distantdeeds.com
Nottingham & Nottinghamshire Victoria Cross Committee		ahigton@aol.com
Afghanistan Trust		www.afghanistantrust.org
Combat Stress		www.combatstress.or.uk
Royal British Legion		www.britishlegion.org.uk

British Limbless Ex-Servicemen's Association	www.blesma.org
RAF Benevolent Fund	www.rafbf.org
Soldiers, Sailors and Airmen Benevolent Fund	www.ssafa.org
Help for Heroes	www.helpforheroes.org.uk
Forces Childrens Trust	www.forceschildrenstrust.org

* 9 7 8 1 7 8 0 3 5 7 2 7 0 *

ND - #0112 - 060826 - C0 - 210/148/6 - PB - 9781780357270 - Gloss Lamination